AF441955

INTRODUCTION

The Bundesliga, first in Mainz and then in Dortmund in Borussia, was Thomas Tuchel's name.

In only nine years, how can you go from bartender to Bundesliga coach? Ask the current Chelsea manager, Thomas Tuchel, who spend a good ten years perfecting his craft on the touch-line with Magnez and Borussia Dortmund and watched the 2019/20 UEFA Champions League final with his PSG side edged by Bayern Munich.

A company defender, Tuchel was a teenager in the Augsburg Youth Academy, but released at the age of 19, never getting the first team.

He then took a brief spell at the Stuttgart Kickers in the Bundesliga 2 before joining SSV Ulm, an exercise at that stage.

He played 68 times, and he was forced to hang the boots up for good at the age of 24 in 1998 because of a serious knee injury. To date, it has been so underwriting that an elite tactician has founded it.

His next move was even more remarkable. Tuchel studied business management at university to prove himself to be competitive away from the football pitch and served as a waiter in a bar in a parallel.

However the football pulley was still strong and the springboard Tuchel was coached by none other than Ralf Rangnick, and RB Leipzig, among others, would continue to be successful. In Ulm, where Rangnick was the lead coach from 1997-99, both formed a strong partnership and Tuchel was eager for one last throw of his dices as a professor after recovering from his knee trauma.

Nine months later, he called Rangnick and then took charge in Stuttgart to call for a trial of the reserves of the club.

But when Rangnick couldn't continue playing in the end due to persistent cartilage damage he sowed the coaching seeds wondering whether or not he could imagine work in youth football. Rangnick was just too glad to compel him.

Tuchel shadowed curiosity for some time before taking over the U14-team in 2000. Curiosity picked up Tuchel for some time. His leg now wedged firmly in the trap, and nobody looked back.

In 2004 Tuchel was promoted as Associate Coach of the U19 and quickly demonstrated his potential in the touchline by helping his sides to win the title U19 Bundesliga the following year, under the guidance of late Mentor Hermann Badstuber – the father of present-day Stuttgart and former Bayern Munich defender Mr Holger.

That triggered a rapid rise in the ladder and just nine years after he waited in a bar, because of his tactical cleverness, his administrative abilities and his ability to identify and seize the chances when they arose he would be first in a dugout at the Bundesliga.

This time as U19 head coach, he returned to Augsburg in 2006, and finished his badges the same year.

Before moving to Mainz, he took charge in 2007/08 of the reserve team and won the U19 Bundesliga in 2008/09, with the future winner of the World Cup Andre Schürrle included. In 2007/08

A well-founded credential, he was threatened both as U21 assistant coach and Hoffenheim as reserve team manager in summer 2009, by German Football Association (DFB).

However, the appeal of the Bundesliga was too strong and he was named as Mainz first team coach on 3 August 2009 after his predecessor, Jörn Andersen, was dismissed following the side's DFB Cup first-round exit to lower-league

outfit VfB Lübeck.

Tuchel took over the reins at Mainz when he was just 36. - 2010

While Mainz was only promoted to the top flight in the previous season, Tuchel led them in his first campaign to a ninth place finish. He began his second term with seven consecutive victories, including a two-and-a-one win for Bayern's German champions.

After finishing fifth in 2011/12, Mainz won for the first time in the club history at the UEFA Europa League, only to be defeated in a third qualifying round by Romanian side Gaz Metan Medias on two sides.

Tuchel became renowned as one of the most tactically clever young coaches of German football during his time in Mainz, constantly changing training courses according to the mission in hand, while still remaining true to his own specific principles.

"There's definitely a style I've got that we brought at the Mainz table: pace forward and attack-minded football," he told Die Zeit, a German publication.

"I prefer some qualities, an active playing style, bold defense and pacy play during attacks."

He also has no doubt that his job will be unorthodox. He once inspired his players to quote Michael Jordan, a legendary NBA: "I've failed over and over and over again in my life. And that is why I succeed." He said, instead of video analytics after a crushing loss.

Tuchel has also contracted a young football hobby analyst, Rene Maric, to scout and evaluate his opposition. Maric was then only an enthusiastic soccer fan, writing his reflections on his blog.

It helped Maric kick off his carrier and he is now assistant to Borussia Mönchengladbach's head coach, Marco Rose. She saw one of his reports and was impressed.

To date, Tuchel remains Mainz' most effective coach in history, having scored more points per game (1.41) than the man who first took them in 2005/06 - Jürgen Klopp (1.13).

Feats like this don't go unnoticed and he spent 12 months sabbatically in Mainz before succeeding Klopp again in this time at Borussia Dortmund after five overachieving years.

There he nurtured young talents such as Christian Pulisic and Ousmane Dembele to become a leading global player and helped BVB complete its career in the Bundesliga in 2015/16 and take side in the glory of the DFB Cup the following year.

And as in the case of Mainz, he became Dortmund's effective coach, scoring 2.09 points per Bundesliga game, before Lucien Favre (2.11) lifted the bar even higher.

In summer 2018 he was named manager of the French giants PSG, winning the Ligue 1 title for his first season, and was just two seasons long in Dortmunder nine years after he was first appointed head coach.

The next season he helped with the domestic treble and, while his first ever Champions League final in Bavaria had been missed, with a higher upward trajectory – the Bundesliga-made tactician will have a lot more silverware in his next nine year circle.

CHAPTER ONE

<u>THE JOURNEY STARTED</u>

<u>Who is Thomas Tuchel?</u>

Much more established than Tuchel's player, who at age 25 was forced to retire with a knee injury, is his management career.

Mainz played his first major part, where he took over Jurgen Klopp for five seasons. After a financial dispute in 2014, he left the club. A year later, Borussia Dortmund was hired to succeed Klopp.

Tuchel remained in Dortmund for two years until he was sacked. He was substituted for Unai Emery in Paris in May 2018, but the third League 1 club was removed from its Paris duties in December.

This is the complete story of a soccer manager named "The Professor." who provides a rundown of important events from his childhood to the present day, along with an unspecified biography in our childhood story Thomas Tuchel. Investigations cover his life's beginning, his life's past, and his popularity.

Yeah, everyone knows he has been one of the most ambitious European coaches in recent years. However, only a few think Thomas Tuchel's biography is very interesting. We're starting now, without ado.

EARLY LIFE

Rudolf Tuchel (a retired soccer coach and a housekeeper and dad), who was born in Krumbach, Germany on 29 August 1973, was born to Gabriele Tuchel, his mother.

It was only natural for Thomas Tuchel to instill a football-loving parent in him. When his son entered soccer management, Sir Rudolf Tuchel already had a great deal of experience in sport.

Did you know?... Rudolf Tuchel is accredited to be his son Thomas' first coach and to teach him how to kick a soccer ball. In Krumbach his western German farming home town Thomas Tuchel had his first taste of football. Thomas Tuchel agreed, with the help of his father, who was a football young teacher, to be his first choice as professional aidist.

Thomas Tuchel grew up with an education. He returned to Krumbach primary school. The first recollection of his education can be seen in his schoolfriend Martin Bosch's poetry album in Krumbach.

Then the weight was 28 kilograms and 1,40m. Dream of the Tuchel. According to Augsburger-Allgemeine Thomas Tuchel entered a number of lines in a poetry album at the age of nine.

<u>EARLY CAREER LIFE</u>

In 1979, he enrolled Tuchel in his local young team TSV Krumbach's love for football. Tuchel was a fulfilled child when he played for his local team, which was his father's employer.

When Tuchel joined the club, still with his father, Tuchel started his midfield career with whom he worked a lot.

The Second Career Option:

Thomas Tuchel went to school too, but he played football under the guidance of his aunt. Once upon a time the 9 year-old wanted to become a "rescue helicopter pilot."

Thomas Tuchel's Childhood Dreams – Second choice. Credit for excursion.

Tuchel wanted to become a helicopter pilot as a career backup option, which was why he was training. Nonetheless, Tuchel found time at Krumbacher high school for competition football, which he attended later in a busy schedule of football academy. All remembers the Grandiose Victory in 1987 at the Olympic Stadium in Berlin.

Making continued success in his soccer career saw Tuchel later compromising his education in full pursuance of his career.

ROAD TO FAME

Tuchel took the next step in his career in 1988, a year in which he had a fruitful trial with the FCAugsburg Academy. In his early years with the club as a footballer he was considered a hopeful gift.

When the Going Gets Tough:

Things started badly with time for the Tuchel. He was never in the first team, and he saw the incoherent effects of his days in the club.

At the age of 19, the year he was to be a graduation and a senior footballer, Thomas Tukel was released from the club. It was a disaster for Thomas Tuchel and his family. Tuchel found in 1992 his lack of hope in the FC Augsburg springboarding.

Moving On:

He watched with determination and self-belief in pain and trauma after his release from the game. Tuchel, however, went to the Stuttgarter Kickers, another German team, which gave him his long-awaited beginning.

Another Disappointment:

During his visit to Stuttgart Kickers Tuchel was largely overshadowed by a number of unimpressive works. The club stopped and decided to release it after more deceptive season 1993-94.

Moving On Again:

Tuchel went on again after his second publication. He participated and again agreed with another club, SSV Ulm. Finally, a pleased Tuchel saw an upsurge from poor performance for a long time.

Senior Career Life of Thomas Tuchel:

In his four-year spell, he became a cornerstone for the club until a new disaster came again.

Suffering another Harsh Setback:

In his career Tuchel sustained another hit. This time, he suffered a cartilage injury, not in his work. The fights of Tuchel were all vain for a full recovery. Having struggled to recover from the injury, he was unexpectedly forced to take action at 25. This meant that for just 5 years he played professional football.

"A lifetime dream abruptly disappears," "

In an interview, Tuchel disclosed it once.

Rise to Fame

Life After His Lost Dream:

Not every part of him had Thomas Tuchel allowed to have his damage. As he nurtured his injury, he continued to study economics and football. Between 1998 and 2000, Tuchel also started taking coaching lessons.

At the beginning of this new millennium, Tuchel thought the time had come for his coaching credential. He was active in becoming a young coach with the German club VfB Stuttgart.

Like his dad, Thomas motivated thousands of kids to grow up by remaining a youth trainer as a soccer coach for five years. You remember that? You knew that? There was a mistake. Mario Gómez and Sami Khedira were in charge of the growth of the first team players.

The Forgiver:

The soccer coach returned in 2005 to his old Augsburg club and threw him out. The club leadership decided to make him a coach for the youth team, with the goal of correcting the mistakes. He was later appointed Team Manager for the Augsburg II club, and stayed there for a period of three years until his fame took him to Mainz. At the Mainz 06, Tuchel won the Rheinhessen A-Junior Championship.

As Tuchel has been the heir of a football class of the low standard, the challenge of Mainz as a newly promoted Bundesliga club was hard to achieve. In comparison, the expenditure was small.

Tuchel managed to defeat Bayern Munich in the Allianz arena with Mainz, his unmatched club. He brought them the best possible beginning of a season and the fifth league finish, the highest in his career.

The BVB Fame:

Tuchel has captured the attention of Europe's top clubs in Mainz. He was the only alternative to succeed Jürgen Klopp's charismatic one. He was unanimously graded as the biggest career leap by Dortmund. Tuchel led his team to win the Garman Cup while in Dortmund.

Thomas Tuchel, Borussia Dortmund's German Cup winner.

Tuchel was praised for his focus on player development during his tenure in Dortmund. Ousmane Dembele and Christian Pulisic had become the stars of the youth-cultured teacher.

PSG Chairman Nasser Al-Khelaifi who brought him back to succeed Unai Emery in May 2018, was the adrenalin shot of Tuchel's methods.

AT BVB

Dortmund's career started perfectly with Thomas Tuchel as he thrashed Borussia in the opening corner of the Bundesliga 4-0 at Monchengladbach. Dortmund was again at its most entertaining and famous free-flowing attacking football we saw under Klopp in 2011 and 2012.

Dortmund lined up in the double pivot at a 4-2-3-1 formation exactly as anticipated by the recent Julian Weigl signing next to Gundogan.

In Mainz, Tuchel had a lot of similarity to the way their teams attacked Klopp wrt tactics and.

Counter-pressure was a common theme with both teams. Tuchel encouraged his attackers to fight long times in Mainz, but a more patient build up is preferred with more experienced Dortmund players. It looked like Mats Hummels was back to his best when he began a series of counterattacks.

Gundogan, as the deeper midfielder when Dortmund was in charge, was also an interesting move. The Gundogan always drops between the two centre-backs, creating time and room for the German ball, as visitors in this area were over 2 to 3.

Dortmund took advantage of it because Hummels and Gundogan began to play easily, and with their complete backs driving the Mönchengladbach midfield to the ground, and were vulnerable to attack. Mönchengladbach was too stagnant to fight any challenges with Kagawa's left-wing push and Reus excellent right. Dortmund played rather well and scored the first two goals mainly due to the rapid turn to which Mönchengladbach slowly adapted.

Defending

Mönchengladbach was extremely well suffocated by a high line with the boy Julian Weigl sitting before the defense. Weigl looked amazing for his generation, and Dortmund looked like they made a genius signature once again. The young German displayed her intelligence and class off her cool and composed of a ball.

"I think Barcelona performs outstandingly based on the way the entire team tried to win the ball after a turnover with abandon and passion."

Although Tuchel favored pressing as an essential part of the game in Mainz, pressing was more limited against Mönchengladbach.

Gundogan was the most involved media player in the press when he stormed the opposition. Mönchengladbach fought for some kind of revival and they were a shadow that qualified last year for the Champions League. While they were a little less than prepared, the course of the match was decided by Dortmund's magnificent display.

Even in Mainz Thomas Tuchel has proven himself to be one of the most tactfully versatile coaches to change his preparation even in a match at all times. His study and research before match are popular and his work is second to none in viewing videos and evaluating opposition.

At Dortmund, he seems to have selected a formation of 4-2-3-1, active transformation into 4-1-4-1 with a high backline. He noticed that the constant counter-pressure that we saw early Klopp places a heavy burden on the players over the course of time (We will have to wait and see whether this high line will be repeated against Bayern who have players to run in behind). He wants Dortmund to create from behind which the back will drive the wings forward and overwhelm them.

Kagawa moves widely, so that the striker and the second winger (Reus) can overwhelm one hand, thereby multiplying the transitional options available in the deep playmaker. Although Dortmund is not yet perfect, the League will be even strengthened and fascinating to observe as an exciting challenger for Bayern. This season's battle between Tuchel and Guardiola is the most thrilling management duel.

WHY DID BORUSSIA DORTMUND SACK THOMAS TUCHEL?

Interesting question.

The first point that should be remembered is that Borussia's board was never stated unhappy about the results of the squad.

Dortmund had several issues to contend with, including the loss of a number of first team players. Those were replaced by young players and Tuchel mostly kept up with the performance his predecessor, Jurgen Klopp, had secured.

His contact with the club board seems to have been the main problem.

It was fair practice for the executive to discuss his decisions with the board at the time when Klopp was in charge and vice versa. In Tuchel's opinion, everyone should concentrate on their own tasks and not intervene in the activities of other club employees.

Tuchel also didn't fear disciplining some of the most successful players in the organization. He was unpopular about this, as a result of which some relationships deteriorated.

The peculiar thing is that now, almost a season later, Tuchel is considered to be the future manager for some of the world's largest clubs and these are among its other attributes. Arsenal, Chelsea and PSG are all involved in the discipline and performance of a director in their clubs. Here I have written more on the topic[1].

Finally, both parties seem to regret Tuchel's decision to step down as Dortmund boss. Despite recruiting a talented boss, Peter Stöger, the team performed below equal.

Tuchel has no employment, but would unlikely remain so for a long time. It is predicted that at the end of the season, he will join a super team.

Still, himself and Dortmund fans must be wondering how things might have worked out had relationship between himself and the board had not become so strained.

RELATIONSHIP LIFE

Behind the good boss there is a fantastic lady, as is seen in the beautiful Sissi who was a former editor.

Sissi and her husband Thomas Tuchel had been together in his time in Mainz 05 since May 2009. There were two girls who were born together: Emma and Kim.

Sissi and Tuchel appear occasionally in public. They are only competing at the tennis and local football tournament in Paris-Bercy.

PERSONAL LIFE

You'll be able to get a rundown of Thomas Tuchel's personal life. Thomas Tuchel is described as a "singlesome person" with "rough edges." sometimes.

Thomas Tuchel is also an exceptional public figure and an expert in the absence of a person on holiday. He consciously safeguards his privacy. No interview or public debate is possible, including his wife and parents.

Tuchel has a good methodological approach to life that ensures no casuality.

<u>*FAMILY LIFE*</u>

Trust and sport performance are strengthened with good family support structures. Thomas Tuchel's family gave him that. It all started when Rudolf Tuchel figured out his son's natural talents and abilities.

Thomas Tuchel's parents still live in Krumbach, their German city, with more than 13,000 inhabitants. A city in the rural neighborhood filled with woodland, fields and grasslands. The Tuchel family has built a football niche.

Family Background And Roots:

Rudolf Tuchel may have been one of the very few professional soccer coaches in Krumbach. This means he's paying for good and presumably runs a nice household throughout his time.

Did you know? You knew? In Krumbach, the Bavarian average is high in number of Jews. Thomas Tuchel could implicitly come into being in a Jewish family.

<u>LIFESTYLE</u>

Tuchel has never been the kind of man since his painful youth who lives in the sophisticated lifestyle easily visible by some lovely cars, swaggers, bubblers and a great home.

While the German-born coach lives a modest life with a wealth of 7 million dollars with Borussia Dortmund & Mainz 05 and now have a net value of around 7 million Euro. He seems closed in his social life for the outside world

<u>UNTOLD FACT</u>

Being a football manager has to be a hard presentation. Tuchel is also confronted to the burden of developing/babysitting modern young players. The hot football game, as seen from the video below, is a chuckle with its touch-line anticorps.

<u>HIS TACTICAL PHILOSOPHY</u>

In this segment, the name focuses on the lesser-known young people of this lovely sport and blends it with a tint of tactical flavor for the enthusiast in football, but I noticed a major gap between them. This mini series focuses

therefore on not too old managers (less als 55 years of age) and their tactical theory. In this work, I offer a detailed view of the new boss of CHELSEA FC – Thomas Tuchel.

Background That's speak

Thomas Tuchel is one of the latest coaches who has never been to the highest degree. He was renamed Krumbach, in a small Bavarian village near Augsburg. At 15 in 1991 and 1992 at FC Augsburg he joined the German Youth Cup twice. Tuchel finished his career as a young man and, on the second level, signed Stuttgart Kickers. But Stuttgart's second season was a fraud because, in its first season, after 8 appearances, it was dropped from the first team.

Afterwards, he joined the SSV Ulm 3rd Division in Ralf Rangnick and was involved in 69 matches for the Swabians in 1998 in six years before his active career was finished because of a symptoms cartilage.

He started his physical apprenticeship and studied English and sportive sciences, but had to quit as a footballer due to a double workload. After finishing his football career, he graduated in business economics.

TACTICAL PHILOSOPHY

As Tuchel explains his philosophy on football, he primarily talks of Barcelona and Pep Guardiola. But Iniesta and Busquets don't really like him. However, Tuchel admires the modesty and determination of those mega-stars who do not think that their usual counter-pressures will take extra kilometres.

Every Tuchel team specifically features the use of offensive counterpressure in the opposing half. Tuchel asked its players in Mainz to play long and easy goal players. Either they straightened the ball or instantly went in counterbalance mode.

"I think Barcelona's excellent performance, based on how the entire team tried to get a ball back after a turnover with abandon and passion" (Tuchel, 2009)

Tuchel does not have much time to offer his suggestions. He can direct young players, develop diverse strategies and styles of play. However, when he joined the Mainz Bundesliga team, he was mindful of the limitations of players. Tuchel started to develop easily understood techniques.

He represented essentially opposing classes, which means, with strict man-orientations, he had 4-1-4-1 against 4-2-3-1 or 4-1-3-2 for 4-1-4-1.

Later, the 4-1-3-2 was progressively turned into his favourite scheme. Diamonds in the middle sector have familiar strengths and disadvantages.

Four central midfields can manage the park's middle, and the opponent is out of number near the ball. The full back usually has a lot of space, but Tuchel was able to make some adjustments so that the center center – inside or outside, to the right – would easily move towards that specific back, close to the opposite back, that the free space on the external lines could then not be used. In the meantime, number 10 has been requested to maintain both opposing   central   midfields.

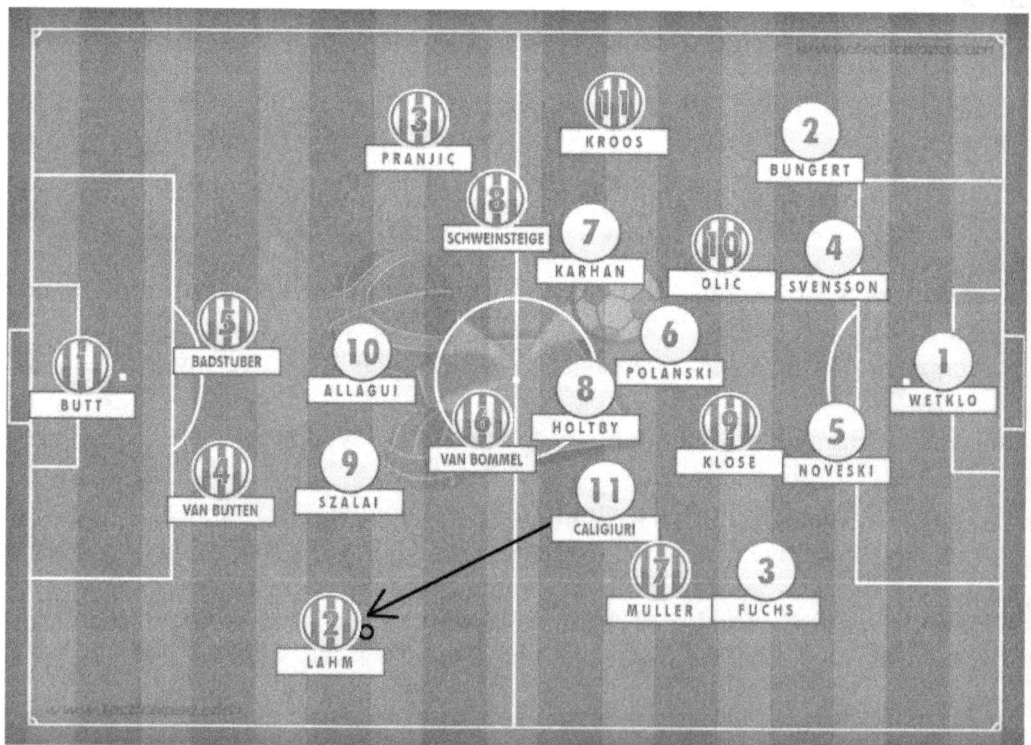

The opening seven straight matches of Mainz 05 were successful, including winning Bayern in the Allianz Arena on 25 September 2010 in Louis van Gaal.

Mainz was able to adjust Tuchel's midfield diamond to defend the putatively exposed wing areas.

One of Tuchel's strong features is that he can react to the tactical setup of the opponent easily. His contributions are not dictated by the availability of his eleven best players. For the sake of his match strategy some players are still left to the table. They're offered up.

Often when they played under Tuchel, great talents like André Schürrle were also lined up. In some ways, regular rotation – particularly tactical – contributed to the growth of almost all players.

Tuchel has been a teacher in the past few years and has been praised for a reason. His pre-game preparation is particularly striking. Often it switches preparation and expertise on community tactical set-ups by watching video material extensively with information collected by other teams. In addition, this approach does not end when a referee blows the opening whistle.

In the 90 minutes, Tuchel reveals the inner Guardiola and rapidly switches training courses and takes individual positions into account throughout the game. The confrontations with Bayern Munich in particular unleashed Tuchel's very best as his teams have taken the superior opponent to the line repeatedly.

For example, Mainz lost 1-4 at the Pentagon at the Allianz Arena in October 2013. (5-2-2-1). However, the match itself was not so significant. Obviously Tuchel was trying to cut down the middle strain, where Bayern was generally able to pass the ball quickly and precisely.

Mainz was therefore able to lead Bayern towards the wing by connecting a full-back left or right center to secure attacks in that area, and then overpower the wide situation. Some of the midfields have turned to the ball to narrow the space of the ball carrier and retrieve it. On the break, the fast-running pack pushed one pivot towards the front. But, as good as this was strategy, Bayern found a hole in Mainz's game. Munich overloaded the deeper spaces with an emphasis on exploiting the lack of pressure in those areas.

Mainz had no nervousness to leave the central midfielder near his foot, so that Bayern could circulate the ball easily and Mainz's defense was overwhelmed. Tuchel is impressive, but still not fine.

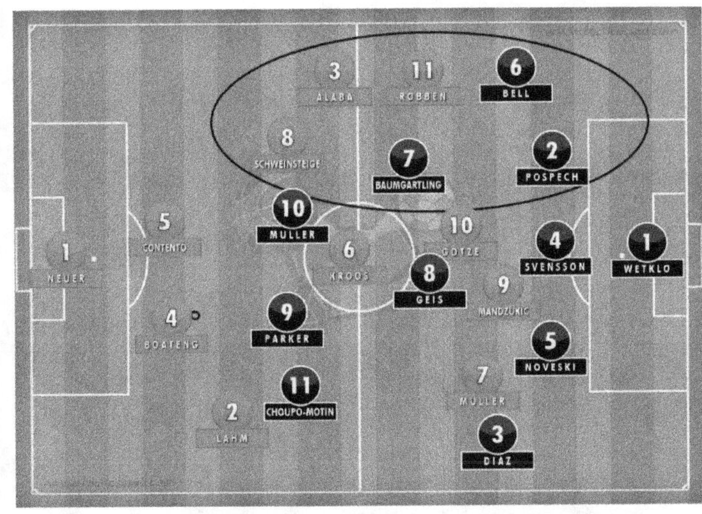

Mainz 05 October 19, 2013: Tuchel defeated Guardiola. The deeper spaces were overloaded by the Bayern 5-2-2-1 type.

The 4-1-4-1 that we saw with Borussia Dortmund in his first pre-saison friends is another training. After Jürgen Klopp left the club, Tuchel's challenge became obvious. He needs to recreate Ball Play game from Dortmund, as the slogan Gegenpressing has recently been battled by Klopp as the best playmaker. In the first matches in the pre-seasons Dortmund was forced to battle physically in the last few seasons by a calmer flow of balls and a lack of useless long ball.

The principle of build-up play is simple to describe: First the ball must pass to the central center midfield position, which plays one-two in front of it with one of the two attacking midfields (number eight). Once Dortmund secures some space, there is one boundary overwhelmingly approaching, one attacking midfield moves widely toward the zone while the single striker fills up in the middle the deserted space. Certainly Dortmund is not ideal at this moment, but Tuchel recognizes the shortcomings again, and seems to be able to fix them.

When Reus was going backwards, BVB overloaded right halving space and extended areas. 6-0 Kawasaki frontale: BVB overloaded. Bourgeoisie Dortmund In Dortmund there were breakthroughs on the side and then decreased in order to find Reus in the centre.

Tuchel hases longlines profoundly, particularly when the ball bounces and nearly mechanically falls down. Consequently, Tuchel modified the shape of the Mainz training pitch.

He cut off the corners and forced his players to pass the ball diagonally. He just switches over and over one of the little twists.

"We learn a lot of ball possession under Thomas Tuchel. Everything's very detailed. How should I move the ball?" Defender Neven Subotic. With which foot should I receive the ball.

A major aspect of his success as a relatively young coach was Tuchel's work at the training pitch and gym. He frequently explores different subjects with scientists. For instance, Wolfgang Schöllhorn, a Mainz-based neuroscientist, used medical findings for his teaching purposes. Tuchel does give up his workout, but plays with various fitness techniques with different guidelines. The players had to adapt to the different training paths and space sizes of the 18 meter x 75 meter wide and 30 meter wide x 70 meter.

It aims to push the players beyond their mental and intellectual limits so as to prevent them from being too trained in competitive matches.

Tuchel is a talented student and a true student of sports. A person who doesn't play the same old book but attempts to write a new book.

In my life, I have been struggling over and over again. Tuchel wrote the inspiring words of Michael Jordan, when Mainz dumped in 2011 from UEFA Europa League towards the Gaz Media AS. "We're successful in that!" "After my career, I have missed over 9000 shots and nearly 300 games I have lost, twenty-six games.

THREE CAREER DEFINING MATCHES

Be the clear underdog against Dortmund's under-19 team, Mario Götze, Tuchel and Peter Hyballa. In 2009 he won the German Youth Championship with Mainz 05 in the finals against his new club and was trained like no other. Her 'game plan,' which Tuchel used to characterize her approach to constantly adjusting to the squad of opposers, was unbeatable that morning.

"You must be brave, you don't need anyone to hide,"

Tuchel said that before his squad left the locker room he was fully committed to beat Bayern Munich.

Tuchel gained three points against German soccer's powerhouse in a third Bundesliga game of August 22, 2009. For the first time, he asked on the big stage what he could do.

He's one of his career matches already ahead of him. The Signal Iduna Park could mark the milestone in a new era as Borussia Mönchengladbach faces Dortmund in the first part of the upcoming Bundesliga season.

THREE KEY PLAYERS DEVELOPED

André Schürrle belonged to the 'Bruchtweg Boys,' named after the old Mainz stadium. Since then, Tuchel and Schürrle had known each other very well, both in the Mainz Youth Section until they went up the ladder. Schürrle's stamina and speed were completely compatible with the Mainz attack, which provided the breaking up of several of the Bundesligas with a continual challenge.

Tuchel wasn't thought to have a big favorite front goal player.

However, Ádám Szalai, 6 ft 4 and 9, was an integral part of Tuchel's Mainz years. However, the fact is that Szalai, who moved from Real Madrid into Mainz in early 2010 is stronger than an extremely good physics.

In 2013, because of his tactical intelligence and agility against a person of his age, he was almost irreplaceable.

When Andreas Ivanschitz spoke about tactics, he was one of Tuchel's outstanding students after entering into Mainz at the same time as Tuchel.

Austrian midscale technological accuracy with great vision and a target nose has been merged. It is strange enough, as his contract had not been extended, that he had to leave Mainz after 104 matches, scoring 22 goals and helping 18 people.

AT PSG

Thomas Tuchel came across enormous problems with Paris Saint-Germain in 2020 for a first-class Champions League finals, Zsolt Low said.

Thomas Tuchel was seen over-even at Paris Saint Germain this season and was not sacked, according to his assistant Zsolt Low.

Finally, PSG announced Tuchel's dismissal after Tuesday's speculative days and ended his 2,5-year stay in the Parc des princes.

The German coach has been rewarded Back To Back in two full-long campaigns, Ligue 1, Coupe de France and two Champions Trophies.

Tuchel led PSG to the 2019-20 Champions League finals, where they were beaten by Bayern Munich 1-0.

However, his ties with Sports Manager Leonardo were broken when he had publicly called the Club Chief of Transfer over lack of spending this season.

PSG lost four out of its first 17 league matches and struggled to resolve a variety of injury problems and the absence of pre-season activities. In mid-season, Ligue 1 split up.

But the two teams, Lyon and Lille, who had advanced from the Champions League to the last 16, struck four to five in Strasbourg and were just one point behind the top two sides.

Low described the specifics behind the sacking of Tuchel and the timing of decision was a shock.

"We were surprised because on December 23, after winning a match 4-0 against Strasbourg, Leonardo brought us together to say that the club was no longer counting on Thomas for the future," he told Nemzeti Sport, a hungarian outlet.

"After the severe difficulties in 2020 and PSG's historic performance, the Champions League Group Phase and the full team swing in the Ligue, the decision was very hard to grasp.

"We were plagued by several injuries during the entire season and had to deal with COVID-19.

I think that completing the year as we did was a great professional achievement. That's the reality we did overdo."

Tuchel appeared attacking PSG in an interview on the day of victory in Strasbourg, acknowledging that the club was more of a "politician" than a managing director.

When she was shocked, Low admits that the tense link between Tuchel and Leonardo meant something inevitably to be done.

He said, "We were surprised," "The Summer window wasn't as we wanted, and after the Champions League run, the bigger players left weren't correctly replaced.

"This created friction among some members of the board and employees as well as the sports manager who adopted different standards of administration than the coach.

"I wouldn't want to go into the details, they had different concepts in various areas and over time the difference of view grew.

"To be honest, this situation should not have lasted. Nearly at the summit, a vast majority of wonderful memories had best be bidden goodbye. If he didn't, Thomas would've not conflict with my principles.

He added, "Formerly, I had the occasion to take over the management positions in Salzburg and in Leipzig and I have not taken advantage of those opportunities.

"If I fought with anyone, it was better or bad. He held his promise, he relied upon me, which is why I felt part of my achievements. Thomas and I had an extreme profession.

"There are also failures. Two and a half years ago I arrived at PSG, and was always with him."

CONCLUSION

Thomas Tuchel has an outstanding reputation as a unique tactician, if an abrasive personality, in Chelsea.

Two primary jobs in his curriculum vitae – Borussia Dortmund, then Paris Saint-Germain – ultimately led him to confront history with his wish that he had total control upon each part of the operation.

And yet, in retrospect, we see that both Tuchel clubs took the hunt for success very close to them. German coach Thomas Tuchel is considered as one of the greatest footballers

Frank Lampard was fired on Monday morning after a torrid league form

In Dortmund, Tuchel couldn't duplicate Jurgen Klopp's Bundesliga titles or refuse an all-conquering Bavarian Munich, but in 2017 he delivered his final piece of silverware, the German Cup.

And in the PSG, whose premise is domestic dominance, he led them to lose the Champions League at the heart of the end of last season only in Bayern.

Although Chelsea and Bayern may not have hoped to get over the road early, Tuchel should be able to lift his new team up over their limited performances in 18 months under Frank Lampard.

Roman Abramovich, the club owner in Chelsea now has Tuchel to impress.

Tuchel, 47, is known for being creative and tactical in improving young players.

His arrival at Chelsea – on Wednesday evening he could be at home with the wolves – seems to be an accident in large numbers expecting it, given the number of managers who came to match Roman Abramovich's owner's value and goals.

However, Tuchel may also be the perfect individual to restore Chelsea's place as Premier League powerhouses next to Liverpool and Manchester.

A Tactical Shape-Shifter

Tuchel would hardly be on top of Chelsea players if he takes over his first game and does not spend time on preparation.

In this regard, the well-known 4-3-3 arrangement of Lampard or even the balanced 4-2-3-1 defense for most of the Premer League devices is not anticipating dramatic change.

However, after examining Tuchel's strengths and faults, we can expect to see some tinkering in time.

The last silverware for Borussia Dortmund, the German Cup, was delivered by Tuchel in 2017.

THOMAS TUCHEL'S MANAGERIAL CAREER

Games: 447 Games:

Winners: 256 .

Derivations: 112

Draws: 79

Major awards: 7

Managed TEAMS

Augsburg II 2007-08

2009-14 Mainz, Germany

Borussia Dortmund 2015-17

Paris Saint Germain 2018-20

In Dortmund, he began playing 4-2-3-1 or 4-1-4-1 in simple but, in time, he had to play in games three times and gave more room and challenge to the counter.

At PSG, where his team level is slightly higher than other leagues, there has also been more innovation.

From 5-4-1 to 4-3-3, Kylian Mbappe, Angel Di Maria and Neymar used the tutcher to make it suit with a 4-2-2, if he was not wounded. There are at least a twelve separate trainings.

The story is about a football manager who once was intrigued by the salt and pepper shaking around his table at a Pep Guardian Munich restaurants — not afraid of changing things if he did it poorly. He doesn't fear that. He doesn't fear that.

Of course, tinkering will confuse players too much and he will not be as luxurious as he is in Paris. They have to desperately start winners and the Premier League is notoriously stubborn.

Players Need To Think For Themselves

With the physicality of the players and also the psychological skills tested, Chelsea training sessions take on new intensity.

Their need to think quickly when playing high-pressure games is an important feature of Tuchel's demands.

His players and his defenders, in addition to him, need to react quickly to the scene and decide correctly rather than provide a lot of instructions.

After nearly losing PSG in the final Tuchel consoles Neymar last season's Champions League.

To mimic near spots, Cobham Training pitchos should be divided into sections of different lengths and widths to emulate the shape of game scenarios. It is up to the players to make a difference.

Initially, Tuchel had refused to take on a new role halfway through the season since she left PSG just last month and the adjustments in that respect can be slow due to a lack of preparation time for this particular campaign.

Pick 'N' Mix Philosophy

While not much younger than any of them, during his entire career Tuchel trained similarly to Guardiola and Jurgen Klopp.

But his technique is not a precise imitation of any of these famous coaches but rather a mixture of preference.

The players of Chelsea expect the opposition to be big - possessions indeed are the same as strength - but not Klopp's "Gegenpressing" slavery, which requires endless activity and devotion from all.

Similarly, 80% owning, as the teams of Guardiola and the other side are bogged down in a blurred passage, is not necessary. The Tuchel Chelsea won't be any counter-attacking faction like Manchester United.

It's somewhere in the middle of the three. Following Klopp's success in Dortmund in 2015, Tuchel turned from hard work by Sven Bender to better ball control by Julian Weigl in the centre.

Who Will Be The Midfield 'Pivot'?

Weigl and Gonzalo Castro were the centerpiece of Dortmund around which everything else had revolved. Weigl was a deep dramatic, while Castro was box-to-box.

Then Tuchel brought Raphael Guerreiro in the summer of 2016 mainly for his ability to dribbling.

In Chelsea, the obvious 'gateway' is at least Jorginho now and the adaptable Mason Mount might play Castro's part in the Box-to-Box.

For now, Jorginho might be Tuchel's centerpiece, but a new signature is important in the summer.

He did a job such as the PSG pivot, and was half-fit for the Champions League finals.

The problem is that there is no substitute for the N'Golo Kante industry which has to afford Chelsea a chance.

Tuchel needs preferably someone who can hold his own pass, but still spray it.

All Is Not Lost For The Academy Graduates

The general view is that Tuchel's arrival will be a great news for the costly and bad summer arrival, Timo Werner and Kai Havertz.

His appointment is therefore devastating for graduates such as Mount and Tammy Abraham who have praised Lampard for their faith.

The belief, however, that the German vernacular will be chatted by Tuchel waltzes, Werner and Havertz, and will favor them forever is misled.

Although Werner and Havertz will definitely benefit from a coach who is thoroughly influenced by German clubs, Tuchel has a good record of young people's success.

Dortmund's best soccer was played by Ousmane Dembele far from the injury he has been spending since then in Barcelona.

He played with young players and got the best of Ousmane Dembele

It was the same with Andre Schurrle and Lewis Holtby, who finished fifth and finished in the European competition in 2010-11, who were emerging in the management team at Mainz in the first time.

Mount, Abraham, and all the other Chelsea Academy graduates have left the impression that perhaps not Lampard's departure has to be taken into account.

Good News For Strikers

Werner's confidence has diminished in the wild scoring in the Premier League going back to November.

Although Luton lost his mood during his finals in Lampard on Sunday in the third round of the FA Cup against League Two Morecambe.

International Germany has recognized its £47 million prize tag plus physical demand for play in England, despite Chelsea's promising launch.

Cosy summer signatures are being battled and given priority to Kai Havertz (left), and Timo Werner, both German.

The fall man of the departure from Lampard is considered to be Mason Mount.

The good news for Werner is that Tuchel still seems to raise the hitters to an unprecedented level of score.

In his first season as managing Director of Dortmund, Pierre-Emerick Aubameyang scored 39 times in all competitions and significantly improved with a net of 40 times the year after.

Mbappe scored 39 goals in the first season as manager of PSG (2018-19). Despite the campaign for the League 1, he scored 30 last year, 11 games were earlier shortened because of the Covid-19.

There's something about him that Tuchel gets the most out of his middle.

Complete Control

It will possibly happen in summer when it lists transfer goals that the true test if this works for Tuchel and Chelsea.

With Lampard retired last summer to the first recruitment room after spreading £222m on Werner, Havertz, Ben Chilwell, Hakim Ziyech et al.

It's only right that Tuchel expects cash to form the squad when the next window arrives.

Don't forget that Dortmund sacked Tuchel a short time after they had come to Fina, a famous Champions League, after the conflict between CEO Hans-Joachim Watzke and PSG hierarchy

Tuchel was sacked by Borussia Dortmund after a setback in the transfer plans in 2017

In the past, he also attempted to monitor all aspects of the club's operation by scouting, learning, eating and even infrastructure improvements.

He dropped into a shape while he was in Dortmund when players looked out and prevented him from practicing with Scout Sven Mislintat.

Tuchel went to Watzke and Sports Director Michael Zorc directly for his own players' shopping list.

The rest of this year in Chelsea, if Tuchel had his hands entirely steered them, could thus prove peaceful before the storm.

The very freedom he obtains will perhaps depend upon his success at Stamford Bridge.